MASTERING
MICROSOFT
ONEDRIVE

**Your Ultimate Guide to Exploring Microsoft OneDrive
Cloud Storage**

Sophia Ryan

TABLE OF CONTENTS

CHAPTER 1

INTRODUCTION TO MICROSOFT ONEDRIVE

OneDrive, originally named SkyDrive in August 2007, has transformed into the current cloud storage platform. This tool facilitates document sharing and collaboration, also functioning as a cache repository for Microsoft's remote Office apps.

In addition, OneDrive serves as a storage repository, prompting users to upload and secure their documents on Microsoft's cloud servers. Professionals favor it for storage services because of its competence in consolidating, distributing, collaborating, and organizing records. Users possessing a Microsoft account can utilize OneDrive.

DEFINITION OF ONEDRIVE

Open to all Microsoft account holders, OneDrive is a widely accessible online storage solution. Users might conceptualize it as a connected storage facility allowing sharing with minor fees. As a Microsoft cloud service, OneDrive introduces users to an extensive digital library, empowering them to exercise caution in securing their data and keeping it separate from other accounts. With an initial 5GB of limitless storage, users can expand to larger capacities as needed or for enjoyment. Its seamless integration with Microsoft Office facilitates convenient editing and sharing of documents in Word, Excel, and PowerPoint.

OneDrive offers protection for your files, employing explicit coding to thwart unauthorized access. One of its standout features is the capability to synchronize users' data consistently across all devices, including Android and Apple mobile devices.

WHY SHOULD YOU USE ONEDRIVE?

The extensive popularity of OneDrive can be traced back to its multitude of positive features below:

1. **Accessibility**: OneDrive can be reached from any computing device, allowing account holders to retrieve their data from anywhere.
2. **Security**: OneDrive employs various methods, including obfuscation, to safeguard your collections.
3. **Collaborative Editing**: OneDrive simplifies and enables the seamless transfer of collections among users.
4. **Synchronization**: OneDrive keeps client libraries consistently updated by utilizing your machine devices to duplicate files across them.

BACKUP YOUR FILES

The necessity of file backups is profound and holds substantial importance. Retrieving certain files and folders for tasks can become a challenging endeavor for users without a backup.

Follow the provided steps to create a backup of your files:

1. Open OneDrive by selecting its icon in the menu bar.
2. Compile a list of the specific documents or files you wish to back up.
3. Set your preferences accordingly.
4. If opting for a specific collection, use the control-click function to choose "copy to OneDrive."
5. Allow the files to load and update automatically. This concludes the backup process

Furthermore, we will explore the process of backing up an Android phone or any other type of computing device to Microsoft OneDrive:

It is prudent to acquaint oneself with backup procedures in the event of unfortunate occurrences such as phone malfunctions or the sudden loss of computing devices during critical moments. The repercussions of such regrettable situations can result in the loss of many valuable items. Unused data and collections, including photos and memos, are prone to disappearing, and the irreversible nature of this loss can be deeply distressing for the user. Therefore, it is highly recommended that individuals take the time to carefully review the following steps to avoid such heart-wrenching scenarios and offer assistance to less informed friends.

Users of Microsoft OneDrive can effortlessly and swiftly store their files on the cloud, providing easy access whenever they desire, regardless of their location or the time. The widespread awareness that Microsoft OneDrive seamlessly integrates with Windows shortcuts enhances its usability for a majority of users.

The compact Android device is well-suited for utilizing OneDrive, allowing you to securely backup your Android data using the platform.

Note: OneDrive consistently backs up data from handheld devices and has made a dedicated effort to support Android. Refer to the steps provided below for guidance on creating a phone backup using OneDrive.

HOW TO BACKUP FILES TO ONEDRIVE USING YOUR ANDROID IPHONE AND WINDOWS PHONE

Ensuring the security of your data involves understanding the process of backing up files, either through OneDrive's specialized drive or an online resource. Once you have installed and configured the OneDrive mobile app, you can start utilizing it for backing up files from your phone. It's important to note that OneDrive provides reliable applications for Windows, iOS, and Android phones. Follow the instructions below to use your phone for backing up files to OneDrive:

Step 1: To get started, users should log in their OneDrive account details

Once the OneDrive app is installed and your device is prepared, launch it to begin using it at your convenience. The user needs to ensure they register with the Microsoft OneDrive Android application using their identity.

The instant you choose the 'sign up' control, you will automatically be able to use this first step to

Creat fresh account.

Step 2: Upload Files to OneDrive

The OneDrive application for Android offers a sleek graphical interface that allows you to either view your existing files or upload new items. Click on the menu icon (symbolized by three dots) located at the screen's upper part to commence a backup to OneDrive using your mobile device.

Various operations can be performed on the Microsoft OneDrive iPhone or iPad application. To back up files from your smartphone to OneDrive, select the "Add Items" option.

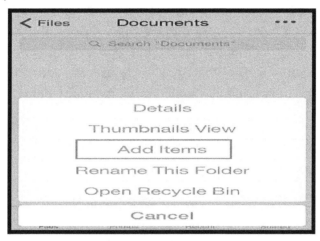

Step 3: Grant Permission and Manage Content

Authorize the Android OneDrive software to access specific information by clicking the "Ok" icon in response to the notification dialog. Proceed to OneDrive, choose the files you wish to back up, and exercise patience as your data is imported. Afterward, you can conveniently modify your files using the app's dashboard.

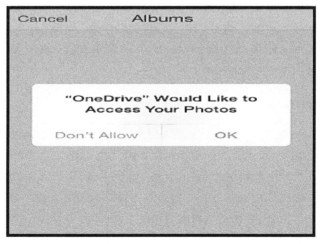

Being informed about the three distinct methods for backing up files to OneDrive allows you to easily safeguard your data. OneDrive provides a dedicated folder, a web interface, and a mobile app for file backups. Experiment with your preferred option today and share your thoughts.

ACCESS YOUR FILES FROM ANY LOCATION

For those engaged in the expanding global workforce, the concern of missing important information is alleviated, as access to your documents is available from any location. Conducting business and staying agile becomes possible whenever you have internet connectivity. Various methods exist for remotely managing your computer, accessing information, and controlling it from anywhere you are. The strategy you choose will depend on how you retrieve files and the tools you have available when away from your workstation.

The simplest approach involves copying all your data from the original location to a portable hard drive that you can carry with you. However, this method can be cumbersome, as it requires setting up the portable drive through your home computer.

In the contemporary landscape, more advanced methods are now accessible. This piece will explore several devices and tools that can assist with this task, regardless of when or where it is needed.

Ways to Access your Files from Anywhere

Step 1: Cloud-Based Solutions for Remote File Management

Utilize cloud computing services, specifically web applications designed for online backup and file synchronization, to remotely access files from any location without the need for additional equipment. Specialized file-syncing software and services ensure that essential documents are always accessible, regardless of your location.

Step 2: Network Attached Storage Devices (NAS)

A NAS serves as a compact remote file server connected to a home network. It proves beneficial for file sharing and backups across multiple computers, typically offering remote file access through FTP or a web browser, depending on the device. Popular NAS options that facilitate remote file access include Buffalo Link Station and Apple Time Capsule. If your goal is solely to access shared files over the internet without the need for remote computer control or management, a Network Attached Storage (NAS) device is suitable.

Step 3: Remote Desktop Tools

Another method to retrieve files from any location with Wi-Fi or internet access is through remote login to your computer. This setup mimics your presence in front of your PC at home, providing remote access to anything available on your computer when you are physically present. While there are subscription-based remote desktop programs, there are also free remote access tools suitable for most users. These tools enable you to view your home files while away, print remote files locally, and transfer files to and from your home computer.

Step 4: Virtual Private Networks (VPNs) and Home Server

If you prefer not to rely on a third-party solution, you can establish a Virtual Private Network (VPN) and set up your own server. While this option is the most expensive and time-consuming to configure—usually involving software costs and the necessity to forward router ports—it provides the highest level of control. For Mac users, macOS Server is an option that simplifies home or small business networking and remote access. Linux offers server alternatives like Ubuntu Server, openSUSE, and Oracle Linux.

On the other hand, there are HTTP servers that are easy to use and can be set up quickly (for instance, HFS, a free remote file server program compatible with Windows and Linux). If FTP is your preference, there are various free FTP server programs at your disposal.

HOW TO SHARE AND COLLABORATE FILES

The content stored in your OneDrive is kept private unless you decide to share it. It's crucial to understand that when sharing folders with Edit permissions, the recipients can integrate the shared folders into their own OneDrive. This enables them to maintain the folder alongside their personal folders, effortlessly move items between folders, and work on it offline for added convenience. Any changes they make are synchronized with the shared folder, ensuring that everyone with access stays updated.

To share files or folders on OneDrive, follow these steps:

1. Go to the OneDrive website and log in using your Microsoft account or your work/school account.
2. Select the file or folder you want to share by clicking on the circle in the upper corner of the item.
3. Click on "Share" at the top of the page.
4. Choose "Anyone with the link can edit" to customize link options.
5. Set the desired options for your link and then click "Apply" when you have completed the customization.

Note: Sharing multiple items simultaneously is not available for OneDrive for work or school accounts. If using List view, click on the circle on the left side of the item. You can also select multiple items to share them collectively.

When using Tiles view:

1. Click on the circle in the top right corner of the item.
2. It is also possible to select multiple items for simultaneous sharing.
3. Choose the "Share" icon at the top of the page.
4. Insert Sharing Settings Screenshot - Version Two

If the chosen file or folder has been previously shared, a Shared with list appears at the bottom. Each entry in the list shows either the profile photo of an individual or the initials of a group with whom the file has been shared. To adjust the access level for a specific individual or group, click on the respective photo or group initials to access Manage Access.

If the currently selected file or folder is not shared with anyone, the Shared with list will not be visible. Click on settings to access the link settings.

Please note that your default settings may differ based on configurations set by your administrator. For example, the button might alternatively display that People in <Your Organization> can edit.

[Insert Sharing Settings Screenshot - Image One]

For OneDrive users within a work or school environment, the option to modify link permissions is accessible. If not, proceed to the next step. Choose an option to specify who you want to grant access to via the link.

If a sharing option is grayed out, it might be restricted by your organization's administrators. For instance, they may choose to deactivate the "Anyone" option to prevent usable links from being shared with individuals outside your organization.

    A. "Anyone" grants access to anyone receiving the link, whether directly from you or forwarded by someone else. This may include individuals outside your organization.

    B. "People in <Your Organization> with the link" allows anyone within your organization possessing the link to access the file, whether received directly or forwarded.

    C. "People with existing access" is employed by individuals already having access to the document or folder, without altering any permissions. This is suitable for sharing the link with someone who already has access.

    D. "Specific people" provides access exclusively to individuals you specify, even if others already have access. If the sharing invitation is forwarded, only individuals with existing access to the item can use the link.

Note: To monitor access and ensure security, sharing is restricted to individuals within your organization or those with a Microsoft Account.

INSTALLING ONEDRIVE

OneDrive is a cloud storage service that enables you to access and modify your files from any device. To install OneDrive on Windows 10, you can follow these steps:

1. Navigate to the Microsoft Store app and search for OneDrive.
2. Click on the OneDrive app by Microsoft Corporation and choose Get. Once the app is installed, open it and sign in with your Microsoft account.
3. Alternatively, you can access your OneDrive files through File Explorer.

    If you already have OneDrive installed, you can check for updates by clicking here.

INSTALLING ONEDRIVE ON YOUR DESTOP PC OR MAC

From Installing OneDrive on your computer (FOR WINDOWS)

1. If you are using Windows 10, your computer already has the OneDrive app installed. If not, you may go to

https://www.microsoft.com/en-ww/microsoft-365/onedrive/download   to
download the OneDrive installer.

Click the Start button, search for "OneDrive", and open it.

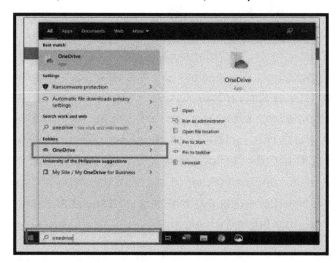

2. To initiate the setup of OneDrive, log in using your Office 365 email, formatted as (password)@outlook.up.edu.ph.

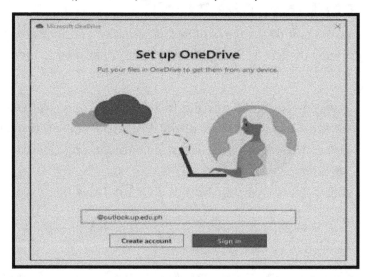

3. On the OneDrive folder screen, click "Next" to approve the default folder location for your OneDrive files. If you wish to modify the folder location, choose "Change location."

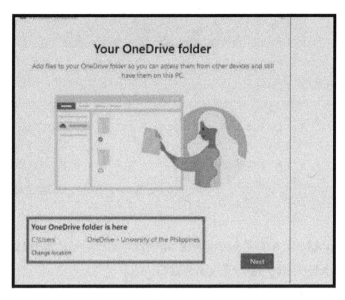

4. On the installation screen, click "Next" to continue. After the setup is finished, open your OneDrive Folder by selecting "Open my OneDrive folder."

5. In the File Explorer window, you may notice the presence of "OneDrive - University of the Philippines." Once everything is set up, all your files will be automatically synchronized to your computer.

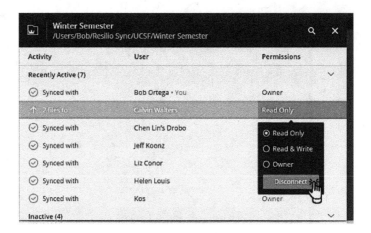

How to Upload Zoom Meeting Recordings to OneDrive Automatically (FOR WINDOWS)

1. Generate a fresh folder in your OneDrive titled "Zoom Meeting Recordings." After your online and computer drives are synchronized, the newly established folder should be available in both drives.
2. Within the Zoom computer application, navigate to Settings (by clicking the gear icon) and modify the destination for your Local Recordings to the recently created folder in your OneDrive.

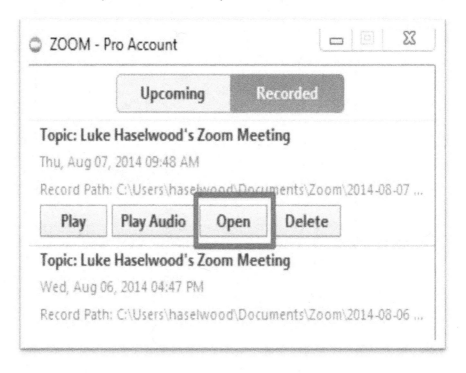

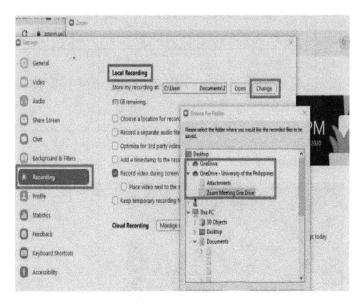

3. Ensure that when recording your Zoom meetings, you save them locally on your computer rather than in the cloud

Installing OneDrive on IOS and Android devices

By utilizing OneDrive on your mobile device, your files remain safe and can be reached from any location across all your devices.

1. Obtain the OneDrive application from the Apple App Store.
2. Log in using the work or school account associated with your OneDrive to access and share your stored files.
3. To include another account, such as your personal OneDrive account, select the Accounts and Settings icon (represented by an iPhone profile icon) and then choose Add account.
4. If you have the Office mobile apps, such as Word, Excel, or PowerPoint, you can also open, view, and edit your OneDrive files directly from those applications.

Setting up OneDrive is a fast and straightforward procedure that only requires a few minutes. This article will guide you through the process, starting with the installation of the OneDrive app on your Android device:

1. Download OneDrive from the Play Store.

Microsoft OneDrive

Developer: Microsoft Corporation

Price: Free ★★★★★

2. Open the application on your phone and enter your Microsoft account login details.

Protect your files and access them anywhere

SIGN IN

NB: You have the option to establish a new account if you are using OneDrive for the first time. Alternatively, if you prefer not to sign in immediately, you can grant permission to view all your photos within the app.

3. Upon accessing the Home tab, you will encounter files from your OneDrive. In the case of a newly created account, it may initially be empty. You can utilize the "Take a Tour" feature to familiarize yourself with the fundamental aspects

Uploading a file to OneDrive on your Android phone is a simple process.

1. Select the plus button at the top, and a list of options will appear.

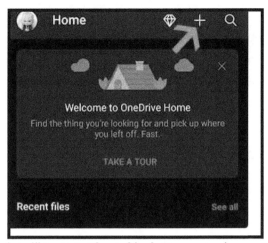

2. Choose "upload" to transfer a file from your phone. You have the capability to upload files with a size of up to 250 GB. Additionally, you can directly upload files into specific folders or sub-folders.

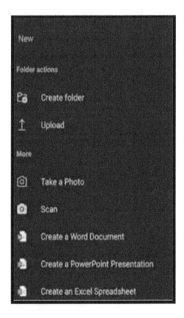

Pricing in Onedrive

OneDrive offers four distinct pricing plans with their respective costs:

1. Microsoft 365 Personal
2. Microsoft 365 Family
3. OneDrive 100GB
4. OneDrive 1TB

The Microsoft 365 subscription, priced at $6.99 per month, includes 1TB of OneDrive storage and Microsoft productivity software like Word, Excel, and PowerPoint. For the Microsoft 365 Family plan, the monthly fee is $9.99, encompassing 6TB of OneDrive storage, productivity software for up to six users, and additional features.

The OneDrive 100GB plan costs $1.99 per month, providing 100GB of OneDrive storage. Lastly, the OneDrive 1TB plan is priced at $6.99 per month, offering 1TB of OneDrive storage.

Carefully review the diagram to observe the different prices based on storage capacity.

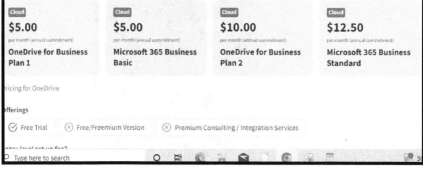

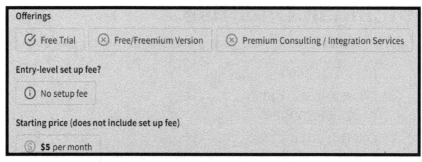

GAINING ACCESS TO ONEDRIVE

There are various methods to access OneDrive, offering users flexibility in their choice. They can opt to download the OneDrive software, visit the OneDrive web interface, or utilize the built-in OneDrive feature in Microsoft operating systems. Refer to the following guides for additional assistance.

Accessing Personal OneDrive Files:

1. Click on the File Explorer icon.
2. Select OneDrive.
3. Sign in to OneDrive if required. Your OneDrive files will be displayed, with folders and files indicating their sync status, distinguishing between offline or online availability.
4. Click on a folder or file to open it.

How to access and manage your files stored in OneDrive on an Android phone?

1. Open the OneDrive application and select the "SIGN IN" option.
2. Input your complete email address and tap the next arrow.
3. Allow time for your folder list to complete loading.
4. You will be shown recent files and additional details pertaining to your files.

Super Useful Things You Can Do with Microsoft OneDrive on

In addition to providing cloud storage space, utilizing the OneDrive software on Android offers numerous advantages. It includes features such as document sharing, photo organization, creating albums, image editing, and browsing through documents.

BECOMING ACQUAINTED WITH THE ONEDRIVE USER INTERFACE

The OneDrive interface is user-friendly and easy to navigate. It features a central dashboard with options for managing documents and files, as well as a control panel with collaborative tasks like adding to and accessing collections. Additionally, it incorporates a search utility to help users quickly and effortlessly locate collections.

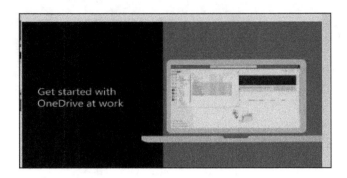

UTILIZING ONEDRIVE.COM

1. Transfer files from your PC or Mac.
2. Collaborate by sharing files with others.
3. Grant permissions to allow others to edit and collaborate on files simultaneously.
4. Access your files from any location, be it your computer, tablet, or phone.
5. Synchronize OneDrive with your PC or Mac to enable access to your files even when offline.

FEATURES OF ONEDRIVE YOU WOULD BENEFIT FROM

The many benefits of OneDrive include:

1. Access files without limitations, at any given time.
2. Makes files accessible for collaboration from any location.
3. Serves as an organizational hub for files.
4. Liberates device storage capacity.
5. Facilitates the sharing of content among teams, regardless of size.
6. Allows for a customizable sync experience (for administrators).
7. Safely stores files and sensitive information.

EXPLORING ONEDRIVE PERSONALLY

If you have OneDrive installed on your computer, the file is already stored locally and ready for editing. Subscribing to Microsoft 365 ensures that any Office file you open is automatically displayed in the online version of Office. For instance, when you open an Excel worksheet, it appears in the online version of Excel in a separate tab, ready for editing.

Similar to a computer file organizer, you can manage your OneDrive files on the web. Hover over a file or folder, and click the circle to select a file. It's essential to click here to choose the file, as clicking on the icon once either opens it or previews it. Standard commands for file management, such as Delete, move to, copy to, and Rename, are visible on the bar. Additional commands can be accessed by clicking the overflow.

The Embed command allows you to embed a live version of specific file types on a webpage. Clicking the generate button creates the necessary HTML code, which can then be pasted into the page. Alternatively, you can right-click on a file to instantly access a menu of file management commands.

All files and folders are automatically synchronized with OneDrive on all your computers and laptops. While manual uploads are possible, adding files locally is generally more effective, unless your local computer is offline or unavailable. A helpful tip is to monitor your OneDrive storage usage in the lower left corner to avoid exceeding your storage quota. If necessary, you may need to purge files or consider upgrading your subscription.

CHAPTER 2

WORKING WITH ONEDRIVE ONLINE

SIGNING UP TO ONEDRIVE

Possible ways on how to sign into OneDrive on a PC

OneDrive comes automatically included with all new installations of Windows 10. However, for users with older versions of Windows, OneDrive may not be pre-installed. If you cannot locate OneDrive using the steps outlined below, it is likely that you need to install it initially.

1. Click on the Start search box or press the Windows key + Q, then type "OneDrive." Once OneDrive appears in the search results, click on it.

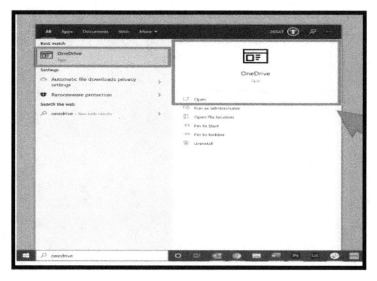

2. If you possess an account, input the email address linked to your OneDrive account and select "Sign in."

If you haven't established a OneDrive account yet, you can either acquire a free account, which comes with 5 GB of online storage, or opt for a OneDrive subscription. You have the option to sign up for any OneDrive plan, including the free one, either on the OneDrive website or by choosing "Create account" within the OneDrive program window.

If you're a newcomer to OneDrive, establish a free account directly from the sign-in page within the OneDrive app. Dave Johnson/Business Insider

3. On the subsequent page, input your password. If you had previously configured two-factor authentication for your Microsoft account, you may need to provide an additional code sent to your phone or email.

4. Adhere to the provided instructions to designate your OneDrive folder. In case you were previously logged into OneDrive on this PC, you might have an existing OneDrive folder. In such a situation, you can simply select "Use this folder" instead.

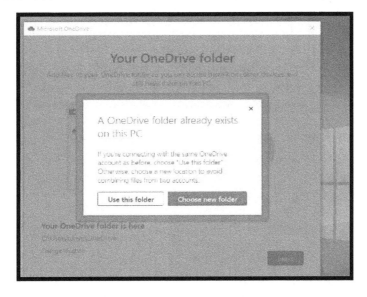

If the OneDrive folder is already present on this computer, you have the option to resume file synchronization using the existing folder. Alternatively, you can select a new location to initiate the synchronization process from the beginning. Andy Johnson/Enterprise Insider

SIGNING INTO YOUR ONEDRIVE ACCOUNT VISIT THE ONEDRIVE LOGIN PAGE.

1. Select 'Sign in' positioned at the top right corner of your screen.
2. Enter your complete USC email address and click 'Next.'
3. If you come across an additional popup asking 'Which of your accounts would you like to access?' choose 'Business.'

Online Interface

An online interface pertains to any software, whether it's a website, a section of a website, or an application, managed by or for an economic entity. Its primary purpose is to grant end users access to the products provided by the economic operator. This definition is derived from information found in 31 documents.

There are two interface types:

1. Graphic User Interface (GUI)
2. Command Line Interface (CLI)

Automatic Syncing on OneDrive:

Users may wonder if OneDrive automatically syncs documents or folders. Indeed, OneDrive does automatically sync files; just make sure the 'Start OneDrive automatically' checkbox is selected. OneDrive will initiate upon signing into Windows, and syncing will commence when there are folders or files that haven't been synced yet.

To manage this on your personal computer, right-click the blue cloud OneDrive icon in the Taskbar Tray, then go to Settings > click the Account tab > choose the Folders link. Select the folders you wish to automatically update across your devices and then click OK.

Personal Exploration of Online Interface:

1. Keep the interface simple.
2. Establish stability and incorporate common UI elements.
3. Maintain focus in page layout.

4. Intentionally incorporate color and texture.
5. Use scripting to create a chain of command.
6. Ensure your system reflects the latest updates.
7. **Systematize standard settings.**

CHAPTER 3

WORKING WITH FILES AND FOLDERS

Streamlining your utilization of OneDrive is a simple procedure. Follow these steps to assist you in generating a folder in OneDrive:

Establishing a new folder:

Open OneDrive and enter your secure access code for accessing the web account.

Choose "+New" from the options and then pick "Folder." Confirm the location within OneDrive.

Assign a name and title to your folder.

Duplicate the URL and either paste it promptly or save it for later use. This enables you to access the recently formed directory in your OneDrive whenever required.

HOW TO CREATE A SHARED, EDITABLE FOLDER?

Discover the process of using OneDrive to create a shared, editable folder, facilitating real-time collaboration on documents and files. To log in to your Microsoft OneDrive cloud account, input your secure code. Be aware that there is a singular option, as well as alternative methods, for establishing a shared OneDrive folder. By following these steps, you can create a shared, editable folder on OneDrive, fostering efficient collaboration among team members on documents and files.

Below are guild lines:

1. Launch OneDrive. Access your OneDrive account by using your preferred web browser, then go to the OneDrive website.

Enter your secure code to access your Microsoft OneDrive cloud account. Note that there is one main option, along with additional alternatives, for creating a shared OneDrive folder.

    A. Activate your OneDrive applications through the settings.
    A. Go to OneDrive.

1. Begin the process by selecting the +New button, and then choose 'Folder' from the available alternatives. Upon successfully signing in, you will be redirected to your OneDrive dashboard. If this doesn't happen, navigate to it manually.

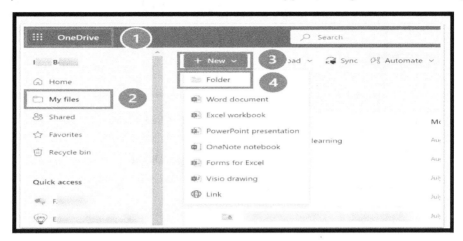

   a. As a precautionary measure, confirm that you are inside OneDrive.
   b. Identify the files relevant to this particular task.
   c. Click on the button with a blue color labeled 'New.'
   d. Choose the icon or button labeled 'Folder.'
2. Give your folder a memorable name Within your OneDrive interface, locate the option to create a new folder.

3. Set the sharing preferences for the folder you've just created.

4. The default accessibility setting is 'Private.' To allow various individuals to edit your newly created folder, choose the 'Shared' sharing option.
5. Modify the folder authorizations through the locations list of options.

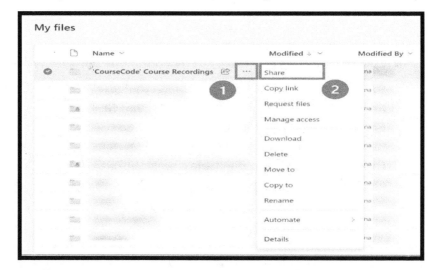

6. By choosing it, you can expand the options menu and click the Sharing button.

RELOCATING FOLDERS IN ONEDRIVE

If you wish to move folders in OneDrive, the process is straightforward. Initially, open OneDrive and navigate to the desired folder. Right-click on the folder and choose "Move." In the "Move Folder" window, a list of available locations to move the folder will be displayed. Select your desired location and click "OK." That's all it takes. The folder will be relocated to the chosen destination.

Follow the detailed steps below for moving a file or folder on OneDrive.com:

1. Locate the file or folder you want to move.
2. Select the specific item intended for relocation.
3. Click on "Move to" in the top navigation.

4. In the Move to pane, find the destination folder and click "Move."

For organizing photos and files in OneDrive, you can efficiently sort, rename, and move them on the OneDrive website after uploading. To access these features, log in to OneDrive on the web using your personal Microsoft account.

To sort files:
1. On OneDrive's web interface, go to My Files and enter the folder containing the files or photos to be sorted.
2. Choose a column header and select your preferred display order (e.g., Name A to Z, Z to A). Alternatively, use the Sort option at the upper right to specify the display order by Name, Modified, or Sharing. Note: The Sort option is available only when signed in with a Microsoft account.

Changing the Name of a File or Folder:

1. Choose the file or folder you want to rename.
2. Click on Rename, and then enter a new name.

Relocating a File or Folder to Another Location:
1. Go to the file or folder you intend to move.
2. Select the item(s) you want to move, and from the top navigation, opt for "Move to."
3. In the Move to pane, find the destination folder and click "Move."
4. If you wish to create a new folder to store the item, select "New folder." In cases where you need to transfer files or folders between OneDrive accounts, such as moving from a Microsoft account to a work or school account, the initial step involves synchronizing the files to your PC or Mac. Afterward, use File Explorer (for Windows) or Mac Finder to carry out the file transfer.

UPLOADING FILES AND FOLDERS

You can store a variety of file types, exceeding 300, on OneDrive through Microsoft Edge or Google Chrome. To upload a file to OneDrive, locate the desired file on your computer, and effortlessly drag and drop it into the OneDrive folder. Subsequently, once you sign in to your OneDrive account, the file becomes accessible from any location.

FOLLOW THE PROCEDURE BELOW:

1. Choose Upload > Files or Upload > Folder.

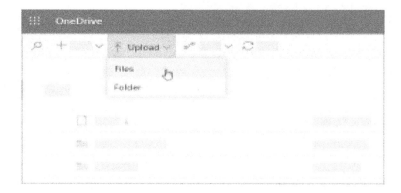

2. Choose the files or folder you wish to upload.
3. Opt for Open or Select Folder to commence the upload process.

Transfer images to OneDrive
How to Move Photos from iPhone to OneDrive?

1. Step 1: Download the app from the App Store.
2. Step 2: Open and sign in using your OneDrive or OneDrive for Business credentials.
3. Step 3: Click on the account icon and access "Settings."
4. Step 4: Select "Camera Upload" under "Options" and click the gear button on the right.

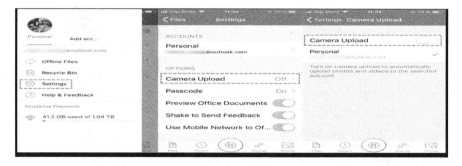

5 Step 5: Confirm to start the process of uploading photos to your selected OneDrive account. Following this, the OneDrive application will autonomously move photos and videos from your iPhone to the specified OneDrive account.

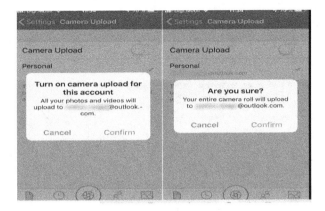

Tips:

1. The initial photo upload to OneDrive may be time-consuming and consume a significant amount of data, so it's advisable to connect your iPhone to Wi-Fi and ensure it is fully charged.
2. OneDrive is capable of uploading photos to only one account at a time.
3. To enable automatic upload of photos and videos to OneDrive, simply activate the "Include Videos" option.

How to Transfer Photos to OneDrive from an Android Phone?

1. Step 1: Obtain the OneDrive Android app from Google Play and install it on your Android device.
2. Step 2: Sign in to the app and tap the "Me" icon located in the upper left corner.
3. Step 3: Navigate to Settings > Camera Upload and activate the gear button next to it.

Step 4: Confirm the OneDrive account where you want to upload photos. Following this, the OneDrive application will quickly move photos from your Android phone to the designated

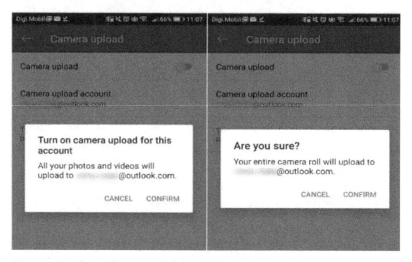

Note: You can choose "Additional Folders" to encompass all folders, including those containing screenshots.

How to Move Photos to OneDrive from PC/Mac using Three Methods

If your photos are originally saved on your computer or transferred from your camera, you can seamlessly transfer multiple photos and various files, such as documents and music, from your computer to OneDrive through several approaches.

1. Log in to the official OneDrive website using your personal OneDrive or OneDrive for Business credentials.
2. Click on "Upload" and locate the photos in File Explorer/Finder that you want to include in OneDrive.
3. Choose "Open" in the displayed window, and the selected photos will be successfully added to your OneDrive account.

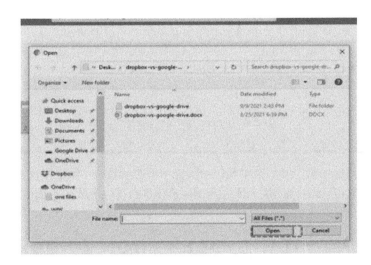

You also have the option to directly drag and drop photos from File Explorer or Finder onto the OneDrive web interface.

How to Automatically Upload Photos to OneDrive Desktop App

Step 1: Download and install the OneDrive desktop application on your computer.

Step 2: Log in to the application, and a OneDrive folder will be generated on your computer.

Step 3: Copy the desired photos for upload to OneDrive and paste them into the OneDrive folder. Your photos will be promptly uploaded to the cloud.

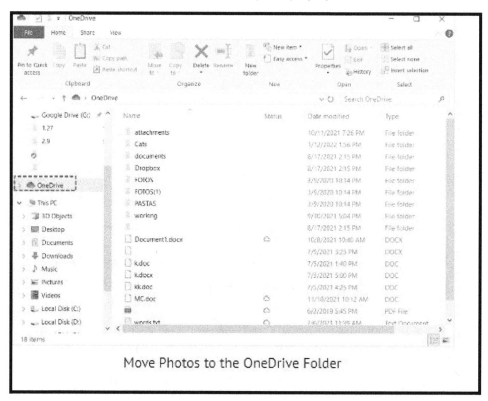

Move Photos to the OneDrive Folder

By opening both the local folder and the OneDrive folder concurrently on your computer, you can effortlessly drag and drop photos from the local folder to the cloud.

DOWNLOADING FILES FROM ONEDRIVE

How to Download All Files from OneDrive?

1. Mark all files and folders, then click the Download button in the toolbar.
2. Utilize the sync option and choose "Always Keep on this device."
3. Employ a PowerShell script to download all files and folders from OneDrive.

Downloading OneDrive Files to Android:

1. Access OneDrive on your phone. Install and open the OneDrive for Android application on your device.

2. Choose the desired files. Select the photos, videos, or files you wish to view and tap the Save button at the bottom.
3. Save the selected OneDrive files to your Android device.

ORGANIZING DATA ON YOUR ONEDRIVE

It is essential to tailor your OneDrive organization according to your preferences. Let's explore the process of organizing OneDrive.

Step 1: Launch the App - Begin by opening the OneDrive app on your device. This application is pre-installed on your phone.

Step 2: Select "+" - Once the app is open, tap on the "+" option located at the top of your screen.

Step 3: Choose "Create folder" - Proceed by selecting the option to create a new folder.

Step-4 Enter name & Click "Ok"

Step-5 Select files & Click three dots

Step-6 Select "Move"

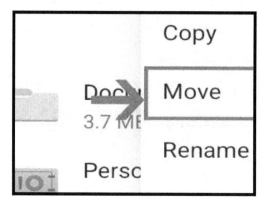

Step-7 Select folder

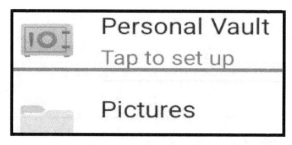

Step-8 Click on "Move here"

COLLABORATING WITH OTHERS ON ONEDRIVE

1. Choose the files or folder you wish to share.
2. Click on the Share option.
3. Opt for "Anyone with this link can edit this item" and configure permissions: Enable "Allow editing" if you want collaborators to edit the file. Disable "Allow editing" if you only want others to view the file.

SHARING FILES

How to Collaborate on OneDrive by Sharing Files or Folders:

After uploading files or folders to your OneDrive, it's easy to share them with individuals or groups. Follow these steps:

1. Log in to your Office 365 account. Refer to the tutorial for assistance.
2. On the top of the page, click the Office 365 app launcher and then select OneDrive.
3. Choose the file or folder you want to share and click on the Share option.
4. In the "Send Link" window, the default setting is "People you specify can view." Click the right-arrow to access more options.
5. In the "Link Settings" window, observe the options, with the "Specific people" option selected. Users can access the files using the link without needing to sign in to Microsoft operating windows, particularly those within UH.
6. In the "Other settings" section, decide whether you want people to edit or download the shared file. Select Apply.
7. In the "Send Link" window's "To" field, type the specific name or group you want to share the file with. As you type, matching options from your contacts will appear.
8. Optionally, provide additional information and then click Send.

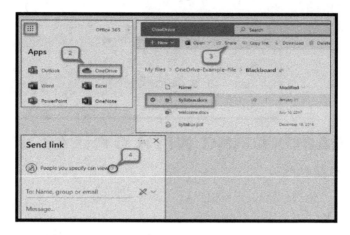

CHANHING PERMISSION ON ONEDRIVE

To change permission on OneDrive, click the steps below:

1. Access Settings.
2. Navigate to Privacy.
3. Select Permission manager.
4. Choose the type of permission to view apps that have the selected permission.
5. Click on an app and choose Allow or Deny.

SHARING FILES THROUGH LINK

1. Choose the file you intend to share.
2. Click on Distribute or Share.
3. In the "General access" section, click Change.
4. Choose "Anyone with the link."
5. Specify the role for individuals with access to your file by selecting an option.
6. Copy the link.
7. Go back.
8. Paste the link in an email or any location where you wish to share it.

NAVIGATING THROUGH FILES AND FOLDERS

To effectively explore files and folders, it's essential to understand the following details.

Firstly, user files and folders are organized in a hierarchical structure, resembling a tree with various branches. The highest level of this hierarchy is the user's "computer" or "personal computer." Beneath the computer, various folders like "Documents," "Collections," "Photos," "Songs," and "Videos" are present.

Follow the steps below to navigate through files and folders:

1. Launch File Explorer.
2. On the left side of the window, you will find folders such as "This PC," "Collections," "Photos," "Songs," and "Videos."
3. Choose the folder you want to explore to view its contents.
4. To locate a specific file, utilize the search icon located at the top of the window.

CHAPTER 4

USING ONEDRIVE MOBILE ON YOUR PHONE

Scanning with your mobile Application

Capturing Documents Using a Smartphone

Have you ever found yourself in need of a digital version of a paper document? For instance, when there's a requirement to swiftly share a document, sending a digital copy via email can be more efficient than using traditional mail or fax. Additionally, having digital copies serves as a reliable backup for important documents in case the originals are misplaced or damaged.

Interestingly, many smartphones and tablets are equipped with built-in cameras that can capture high-quality scans of paper documents. This approach offers a quicker and more convenient alternative to using a traditional scanner.

1. To initiate the process, open the Notes app on your home screen.

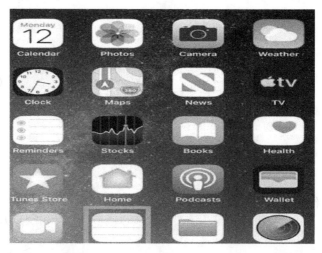

2. Then, select the icon for creating a new note.

3. Click on the circular icon with a plus sign located in the toolbar above the keyboard

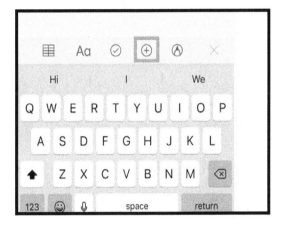

4. Select the option "Scan Document" from the menu.

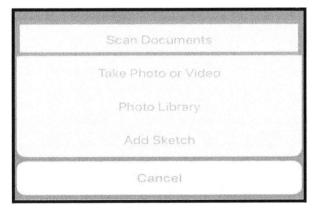

5. Utilize your mobile device's camera to capture a scan of the document by taking a photo.
6. Decide whether to retake the photo or keep it by tapping Done. Then, click Save to ensure the scan is added to note.

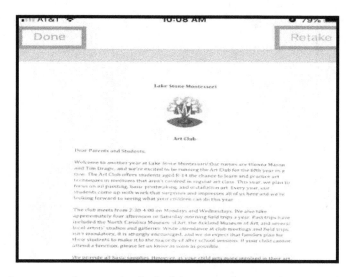

7. The document is now included in your Scanned Documents. To share the document exclusively, tap it to open.

8. Then, select the share icon located in the top-right corner of the screen reveal a menu

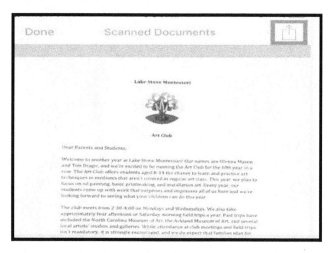

9. Within the menu, you have the option to send the scanned document using your apps, print

   It or generate a pdf

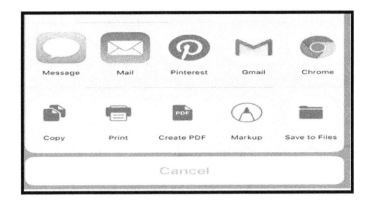

Note:

An alternative method to scan documents using your smartphone involves downloading a dedicated mobile app to your device. These apps have the capability to transform text documents into PDF files. While numerous applications are available, they generally operate on the same fundamental principles. Some widely used scanner apps include Tiny Scanner (for Android and iOS) and Scanner Pro (for iOS). However, you can explore your device's app store to discover additional options.

WHICH TOOLS FOR FILES: SHAREPOINT OR ONEDRIVE?

SharePoint and OneDrive serve as tools for file sharing and collaboration, but they vary in features and purposes. Both being Microsoft products, they enable online file storage and sharing, providing functionalities like version control, collaboration, and security. Nevertheless, SharePoint is primarily a document management system, whereas OneDrive functions more as a personal cloud storage service. While SharePoint is tailored for teams and organizations, OneDrive is geared towards individual users. Additionally, SharePoint encompasses more advanced features, including workflow automation and seamless integration with other Microsoft products.

When to use SharePoint and OneDrive

Comparing the features of both services highlights their distinctions. While both enable online document creation and editing, SharePoint stands out by offering capabilities like the creation and management of libraries, lists, and various content types. Both services support file syncing to computers, but exclusive to OneDrive is the ability to sync files to mobile devices.

As previously mentioned, the primary contrast between OneDrive and SharePoint lies in their target audiences. OneDrive is tailored for personal use, ideal for individuals who require convenient file storage and accessibility from any location. On the other hand, SharePoint is designed for team and organizational use, providing collaborative tools for document management, data handling, and access control.

To illustrate, consider a student needing to store and access schoolwork from anywhere. OneDrive proves to be an excellent tool in this scenario, offering user-friendly features and the ability to sync files across computers and mobile devices. Conversely, for a research team collaborating on numerous documents and requiring version control, SharePoint emerges as the more suitable choice.

The Document circle

Document sets, also referred to as document circles, represent a feature within SharePoint designed for organizing interconnected documents into a unified entity. This proves beneficial for teams engaged in collaborative efforts involving multiple interrelated documents, such as a collection of research papers or a series of legal documents. Document sets in SharePoint serve various purposes, including tracking document status, managing access permissions, and establishing automated workflows for document approval processes.

Moreover, the term "document circle" is employed in document analysis, where a collective effort is made by a group of individuals to systematically read and analyze a document. The objective is to discern and comprehend the document's key ideas, concepts, and themes. The group collaborates to pose questions, engage in discussions about the document, and collectively document their observations.

Document circle in OneDrive

A document circle within OneDrive essentially mirrors the concept of a traditional document circle, but it takes place in an online environment through the OneDrive platform. Participants within the document circle can collectively read and analyze the document using OneDrive's collaborative tools, such as the commenting feature. This facilitates real-time collaboration and discussion surrounding the document.

In OneDrive, the process involves uploading a document and subsequently sharing it with other users. These users can then access the document, providing the ability to add comments or annotations. The document can be highlighted, and users have the option to incorporate sticky notes or draw on the document to emphasize crucial points. Importantly, all these actions occur in real time, enabling participants to observe each other's contributions as they unfold.

EXPLORING ON YOUR OWN

For newcomers to OneDrive, the initial step involves creating an account. Once an account is established, you gain the ability to upload documents and share them with fellow users. Sharing a document is a straightforward process – you simply choose the "Share" option and input the email addresses of the individuals you wish to collaborate with. OneDrive then sends them invitations to access and view the document, allowing them to open it within OneDrive for real-time commenting and note-taking.

OneDrive proves to be an excellent tool for collaborative document work, particularly in scenarios such as document circles, as it supports seamless real-time collaboration and discussion.

In contrast to OneDrive, document circles aren't entities that you can physically "explore." Instead, they represent a methodology or technique for document analysis. To engage in a document circle, you would need to assemble a group of participants, whether it be a class, club, or any other gathering of individuals with a shared interest. Subsequently, the group would collectively choose a document to analyze, employing the outlined steps as part of the exploration process.

CHAPTER 5

WHAT IS ONEDRIVE FOR BUSINESS

OneDrive for Business stands as a powerful tool, fostering collaboration within and beyond organizational boundaries. Its array of capabilities includes simultaneous file editing and enhanced control over sharing, referred to as folder transitions, both internally and externally.

By offering a centralized storage hub, OneDrive for Business streamlines collaboration throughout your organization. Familiarity with file locations enables employees to access them more swiftly and conveniently.

Below are some features of OneDrive for business:

1. **Cloud-Based Repository**: OneDrive for business goes beyond basic storage, offering an extensive array of features. Documents can be securely stored, easily accessed, and efficiently managed from any location using Personal group, enabling seamless remote work management.
2. **Reporting and Data Analytics:** Within the Microsoft productivity suite, there are tools to generate reports and conduct audits for all information stored on OneDrive. This includes data such as the number of documents in use, file views, account interactions, and recycling actions.
3. **Encrypted Data**: Microsoft's OneDrive for business ensures a high level of security for data, whether it is in motion or at rest. Microsoft has implemented an encryption process specifically designed to enhance the security of enterprise data.
4. **File Explorer Integration**: Users can seamlessly integrate OneDrive into their devices using File Explorer for file optimization and management. Data saved on OneDrive can be easily viewed, and data loss can be prevented by syncing known directories with OneDrive, such as document and picture folders.
5. **Simultaneous Editing**: Multiple users can collaborate on the same documents, track changes, and work together in real-time on the same document simultaneously.

6. File Recovery: File retrieval or salvage helps recover documents that have been permanently deleted and ensures the preservation of data stored on the cloud for up to 30 days, even if sent to the trash bin. Accessing deleted previous work is still possible within the specified duration via file recovery.

Utilizing OneDrive for Business enables individuals to conveniently store, share, and distribute their work files within their own cloud-based repository. Each user receives a personalized storage allocation in OneDrive for Business tailored to meet their individual needs. Storing data beyond a user's personal work documents, such as file backups or organizational and departmental data, is not permitted. Assigning per-user permissions to entities like machines, departments, or non-human entities is not supported. For comprehensive content management and collaboration needs, including file storage, communication, and intranet site administration for teams or organizations, SharePoint is the preferred solution.

COST OF INVESTING IN ONEDRIVE FOR BUSINESSES

Utilizing OneDrive for Business eliminates the need to send email attachments and ensures that everyone has access to the latest version of a file. The following is a recent screenshot of Microsoft pricing:

Moreover, OneDrive for Business serves as a cloud storage service tailored for businesses, offering a platform for file retention and collaboration. As part of the suite of office software products, including Word, Excel, and PowerPoint,

OneDrive for Business acts as a secure, centralized hub for businesses to store and manage their documents. By using OneDrive for Business, the need for sending attachments via email is eliminated, and it ensures that all users have access to the most up-to-date document version. Businesses utilizing OneDrive for Business can manage file access, enhancing security through the regulation of user permissions for sensitive data. Within OneDrive, companies have access to tools such as version history and data loss prevention, further enhancing their data protection capabilities.

Accessing OneDrive for businesses

There are multiple methods to access OneDrive for Business:

1. Visit onedrive.com, the official OneDrive for Business site, and log in with your work or school account to gain access. Alternatively, you can open your web browser and enter "onedrive.com/business" into the address bar to reach the platform.
2. If you are a user of the productivity suite, you can access OneDrive for Business through the Microsoft 365 app launcher.

Alternatively, you can follow the steps below to access OneDrive for Business:

- Open onedrive.com using your web browser.
- Verify the legitimacy and security of the site by checking for the green padlock icon and the "Microsoft Corporation" identifier in the web browser's address bar, indicating a partnership between Marquette and Microsoft.
- Gain entry by signing in with your business suit credentials.
- On the Home page of the productivity suite entry, click on the OneDrive option.
- Once you are on the Documents page of your OneDrive for Business, proceed to locate the specific files you need.

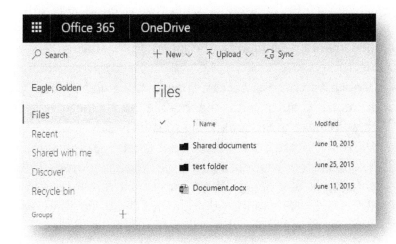

Moreover, the ability to access OneDrive for Business depends on having both an Office 365 account and an internet connection. Once you have these prerequisites, you can visit onedrive.com and log in to gain access to OneDrive. Your files are accessible through the OneDrive application, available on your computer, phone, and tablet. Upon successful login, your documents become visible for access and viewing. Subsequently, you can create, edit, and share files as needed.

EXPLORING ONEDRIVE FOR BUSINESSES

Our journey into OneDrive for Business commences with an exploration of the website's functionalities. Upon logging into the OneDrive website, the main menu on the left side of the interface serves as a navigation hub. This menu allows for swift access to files, shared content, recently viewed documents, and more. Additionally, the search bar positioned at the top of the screen provides the ability to search for specific documents or folders. Once the desired file or folder is located, a simple tap initiates its opening, granting the freedom to view, modify, and collaborate on the file.

For a more comprehensive understanding of the extended features and functionalities within OneDrive for Business:

OneDrive for businesses offers various features to enhance work efficiency:

- File Sharing: This feature enables you to target specific individuals or groups for file distribution, providing control over their permissions to modify, comment, or solely observe the documents.

- Office Online Integration: OneDrive is equipped with Office Online, facilitating the online creation, editing, and viewing of Office documents, eliminating the need for installing Office software on devices.
- Mobile App Access: Accessing and editing files via your phone or tablet is made simpler with the mobile app. OneDrive's search feature streamlines the task of finding specific files.
- Version History and File Locking: OneDrive provides version history, enabling the monitoring of file changes over time. File locking safeguards files being edited from concurrent modifications by others.
- Recycle Bin Function: Additionally, OneDrive features a recycle bin function that enables the restoration of deleted files.
- Advanced Security Elements: OneDrive incorporates advanced security measures such as encryption, multifactor authentication, and auditing.

These features collectively contribute to a more efficient and secure work environment when utilizing OneDrive for Business.

WORKING WITH FILES AND FOLDERS

There are key considerations to keep in mind when managing files and folders in OneDrive for Business:

- - Firstly, utilize the integrated editor to create and edit Word, Excel, and PowerPoint files directly within OneDrive.
- - Employ the check-in and check-out feature to prevent others from editing a file while you are actively working on it. You can initiate the file check-out process by accessing the "More actions" menu and selecting "Check out." After editing, checking it back in allows others to make edits.
- - The co-authoring feature enables simultaneous collaboration on a file with another individual. When selecting a file in OneDrive for Business, a toolbar appears at the top of the screen, providing essential editing tools for creating and editing a file. These tools include text formatting, image insertion, multimedia inclusion, and various other functions. An important advantage is that modifications are automatically saved in OneDrive as you progress.

ORGANISING YOUR VIDEOS AND PHOTOS

Simplify the management of your photos and videos with OneDrive **for** Business, which automatically arranges them by date and location upon upload. You can further enhance organization by creating albums and adding tags to your media. This improves the efficiency of searching for specific photos and videos. Utilize the search tool to easily locate media by entering keywords or tags. To create an album, navigate to the "Photos" section in OneDrive for Business, click on the "Create" button, and select "Album." Provide a name for your album, add photos and videos, and then share the album to allow others to view and contribute to it. Tags, acting as keywords, help categorize photos and videos for future retrieval. Select a photo or video in OneDrive for Business, use the "Add tag" button to input a keyword in the tag field. Tags simplify the process of searching through media and can be used to create dynamic albums that automatically organize items based on specific criteria, streamlining your search.

SEARCHING FOR FILES AND FOLDERS

When searching for files and folders, consider the following tips:

- Ensure the specificity of your search terms to achieve accuracy.
- Use distinctive terms likely to be found in the file or folder title.
- Employ search operators like "AND" or "OR" to connect your search terms.
- Utilize the "Advanced search" link for more precise search options.

For searching within a specific library, follow these steps:

1. Begin by using the "Filter by" dropdown to narrow your search to a designated library.
2. The "Refine" panel provides additional options to filter by criteria such as modified date or file format.

Use advanced search operators for effective research purposes. Here are command terms to study:

- AND Operator: Merge multiple search terms to display results that satisfy all specified terms.
- OR Operator: Incorporate results corresponding to any of the provided search terms.
- NOT Operator: Eliminate results containing a specific term.
- Quotation Marks Operator: Search for an exact phrase.
- Less Than and Greater Than Operators: Define a value range; for instance, the "less than" operator can identify files created before a

designated date, while the "greater than" operator can locate files made after a specific date.

- Question mark Operator, Term-Level Operators, and Date-Level Operators: Explore these operators for enhanced search capabilities.

MANAGING TASK RELATING TO FOLDERS

Folders offer an excellent way to categorize and manage your files efficiently within OneDrive for Business.

Generate new folders, transfer files into existing ones, and partake in shared folder collaboration. To begin a new folder, click the "New" button, then select "Folder" Subsequently, assign a name to the folder and select "Create." Moving a file into the folder can be done by a straightforward drag and drop. To commence folder sharing, right-click the folder and click "Share." Then, specify the individuals you wish to grant access to the folder When you opt to share a file or folder in OneDrive for Business, you can specify who has access and control the actions they're able to perform. An alternative is to offer someone viewing rights exclusively, meaning they can see the file or folder but are unable to modify it. Additionally, it's possible to set a termination date for shared files and folders, ensuring they become inaccessible after a designated time.

Additionally, within OneDrive for Business, you have the option to create alerts for files and folders. These alerts will let you know when someone shares a file or folder, when a file is modified, or when a file is deleted. This approach helps you stay informed about the progress of your files and folders. Additionally, you can instantly access your most-used ones by pinning them to the top of your list.

RECOVERING DATA FROM THE RECIRCLE BIN

In OneDrive for Business, the recycle bin functions as a designated folder for storing deleted files and folders. When you delete a file or folder, it is transferred to the recycle bin, where a version is retained for a specified period, adjustable in your account settings. During this timeframe, you have the option to restore the item from the recycle bin. Failing to restore it within this duration leads to its permanent deletion. Users can modify recycle bin settings, such as adjusting the duration items remain before permanent deletion and choosing whether to receive notifications for file or folder deletions. Furthermore, users can decide if deleted documents should appear in search results or be excluded.

It's crucial to note that the recycle bin retains only items personally deleted. Files or folders deleted by individuals you've shared with won't be stored in the recycle bin. Additionally, items deleted from your personal OneDrive won't be preserved in your OneDrive for Business recycle bin.

Follow the few steps below to recover data

To recover data from the recycle bin, first

- ✓ Access the section of your OneDrive for Business account dedicated to deleted files.
- ✓ Locate the specific file or folder you wish to recover and use the "Restore" button to reinstate it to its original location.
- ✓ For desktop app users aiming to restore data from the recycle bin:
- ✓ Open the OneDrive for Business desktop application and click on the "Sync" icon.
- ✓ Navigate to the designated "Sync issues" area and click on the link labeled "View sync problems."
- ✓ Identify the file or folder you want to restore, right-click on it.
- ✓ Finally, select the "Restore" option from the menu.

Using web app with OneDrive for business

Using the OneDrive for Business web app is straightforward and user-friendly. Follow the steps outlined below:

• Navigate to onedrive.com and log in using your work or school account credentials.

• Once signed in, your files and folders will be displayed, easily accessible with just a few clicks. Additionally, you can create new folders, upload files, and make modifications to existing files.

FEATURES OF THE WEB APP FOR BUSINESSES

The OneDrive for Business web app offers various additional features. For instance, you can create a "OneDrive view" to display all files and folders associated with a specific person or team. A "Personal view" can be established to show only the files and folders shared with you. Custom alerts can be set up to receive notifications about important changes in your files and folders.

Moreover, the "Bulk actions" functionality allows you to quickly edit, delete, or move multiple files simultaneously. The "Shared with me" feature provides visibility into files and folders shared with you by others. To use this feature, click on the "Shared with me" link in the left-hand menu. You can also use the search bar to locate specific files or folders shared with you. Additionally, you have the option to merge a shared file or folder into your individual OneDrive for Business account.

Synchronizing with your personal computer

Synchronizing with your computer ensures that selected files and folders are up to date on both your computer and the OneDrive for Business cloud. This is beneficial for accessing your files and folders across different devices. Syncing a folder to your desktop computer means having access to it on your laptop, tablet, or phone. Any changes made to files or folders on one device will automatically update across all your other devices. Initiate the syncing process by opening the desktop app and selecting the "Sync" icon. Then, specify the folders you want to sync and decide whether to sync all files in those folders or only the most recent versions.

UPLOADING FILES TO ONEDRIVE FOR BUSINESS VIA THE FILE EXPLORER

File Explorer, also known as Windows Explorer, plays a crucial role in managing files on Windows systems. It enables users to view, organize, and search for files and folders stored on their computer. You can access File Explorer by clicking the Windows "Start" button and selecting "File Explorer" from the menu, or by pressing the Windows logo key and "E" on your keyboard. Using File Explorer, uploading files to OneDrive for Business is straightforward. Simply open File Explorer and click on the "OneDrive" icon.

From there, click the "Upload" button and select the files you want to upload. Alternatively, you can drag and drop files directly from your computer into the OneDrive for Business window. Once uploaded, these files will be stored in the cloud and accessible from your OneDrive for Business account.

When using File Explorer for business purposes, it's important to keep a few key points in mind:

- ➢ Ensure that you have the necessary authorization to synchronize the folder.
- ➢ Check that the file's size and type meet the compatibility requirements for OneDrive for Business.
- ➢ Note that uploading a folder may take time, depending on factors such as the folder's size and your internet connection speed.

➢ Remember that you can access your synchronized folders even when offline, allowing you to work seamlessly regardless of your internet connection status.

COLLABORATING WITH WEB APPS

Collaborating on research and files simultaneously with individuals who are not physically present can be accomplished through web applications. OneDrive for Business facilitates teamwork on various document types, including Microsoft Office documents like Word, Excel, and PowerPoint. Any modifications made to a file are instantly visible to all others who have access to the file.

Here are methods for collaborating with web applications:

1. Establish a collaborative folder and invite individuals to join.
2. Generate a shared link that directs to a specific document.
3. Create a cloud-based Office 365 team and share files with its members for collaborative work.
4. Utilize Office Online for modifying records.
5. Collaborate on document edits with others using the contributing feature in Office Online.

Key Features that Facilitate Collaboration with Web Applications:

1. Real-time Collaborative Editing: This feature allows multiple users to work together on a document simultaneously, with all edits being instantly saved. There's no need to physically manage the file or deal with multiple copies. It's an excellent way to collaborate on projects created in Word, Excel, and PowerPoint.
2. Revision History: This functionality enables users to view previous versions of a project and restore them if necessary.
3. Comments: Users can annotate documents and respond to comments made by others, fostering communication and collaboration.

4. @Highlight Function: This feature allows users to tag individuals in comments to bring specific attention to them during collaboration.

Using the Skype for Business Platform:

To get started, verify that you have a Skype for Business account and ensure it has the necessary permissions to use the software. Once confirmed, set up the

Skype for Business application on your work machine. After completing this setup,

Starting a Chat:

1. In the document you want to discuss, click "Share" and then choose "Chat."
2. Specify the individuals with whom you wish to have conversations.
3. Enter your message in the discussion box.
4. Select "Expand" from the chat window's menu. The dialogue window also allows you to include documents, create polls, and perform additional tasks. You can also include a chalkboard in your conversation for real-time drawing and collaboration.

Making Calls and Video Conferencing:

Follow these steps to place a call:

- To initiate a conversation about a file, select "Share" before clicking "Call."
- Click the "Call" button next to the preferred contact.
- Specify if you would like to initiate an audio or video connection.
- Choose your preferred camera and microphone settings if opting for video.
- When ready to connect, click "Start Call."
- Users can utilize various options in the call window during the call, such as muting their microphone. This feature is useful when there is excessive noise in the environment or when you don't want others to hear what's happening around you.

Chapter 7

Top Tips and Tricks for Microsoft OneDrive

The term "tips and tricks of Microsoft OneDrive" encompasses a range of methods, approaches, and quick solutions that users can utilize to enhance their effectiveness and productivity while utilizing the Microsoft OneDrive cloud storage service. These tips and tricks often entail leveraging particular features or functionalities of OneDrive innovatively or efficiently to accomplish goals like streamlined file management, improved collaboration, data security, and smooth synchronization across multiple devices.

Here are some valuable tips and tricks to make the most of Microsoft OneDrive's capabilities:

1. Utilize the "File Restore" feature to recover previously deleted documents or files.
2. Quickly access all shared documents with the "Shared with Me" option.
3. Optimize storage on your system by selectively downloading files using the "Files On-Demand" feature.
4. Continuously back up photos and videos from your mobile device or camera using the "Automatic Camera Upload" function.
5. Synchronize your files across multiple devices with OneDrive, ensuring accessibility from any location. Additionally, set up automatic backups to prevent the risk of data loss.

Let's discuss methods for saving space on your computer, particularly using OneDrive for Business's "Free up space" feature. This feature enables you to remove files from your computer while keeping them stored in OneDrive, which is helpful for managing limited storage capacity or decluttering your hard drive.

To utilize the "Free up space" feature in OneDrive for Business, follow these steps:

1. Open the OneDrive for Business application and click on the "Sync" icon.
2. Select the "Free up space" option from the menu.
3. Your device will display a list of files consuming the most storage space.
4. Choose the files you want to remove from your device.
5. Click on the "Free up space" button.
6. The selected files will be removed from your device but remain accessible through OneDrive for Business. You can re-sync them at any time if needed.

Additionally, you can optimize storage further by enabling the "Files on demand" feature:

- Locate the "Sync" icon in the OneDrive for Business program.
- Choose "Settings" from the dropdown menu.
- Navigate to "Files on demand" and enable it.
- Confirm your selection by clicking "OK".

Enabling "Files on demand" ensures that files are not automatically downloaded to your device unless you specifically request them. This can help speed up synchronization and free up storage space on your computer.

Uploading from Your Phone's Camera

Uploading photos and videos from your phone's camera roll to your OneDrive for Business account is an excellent method for both backing up your media and sharing it with others.

Follow these steps to upload photos and videos from your mobile device's camera roll to OneDrive for Business:

1. Download the OneDrive for Business mobile app.
2. Install the OneDrive for Business app and log in with your credentials.
3. Choose "Upload."
4. Select the images and videos you want to upload.

5. Tap or click the "Upload" icon.
6. Your pictures and videos will be uploaded to your OneDrive for Business account.
7. From this point onward, you can access, edit, and share your photos and videos on any device.

Features of Uploading from Phone Camera

One of the most convenient features is the ability to effortlessly upload recent photos and videos directly from your mobile device's camera roll. This eliminates the need to manually upload your pictures and videos each time.

To set up this feature, follow these steps:

1. Open the OneDrive for Business app and click on the "Me" icon.
2. Go to "Settings."
3. Choose "Auto upload" and select the camera roll where you want automatic uploads to occur.
4. Click "Done."

Another noteworthy feature of the OneDrive for Business app is the capability to share your photos and videos with others.

Here's how you can share your media:

1. Click on the photo or video you want to share.
2. Hit the "Share" button.
3. Enter the username or email address of the person you want to share with.
4. Click "Send."
5. The recipient will receive the URL to the uploaded photo or video.
6. The shared content can be viewed or downloaded on any device.
7. The same process can be applied to share an entire folder containing photos or videos.

Additionally, the app allows you to tag people in your photos, making it easier to locate pictures of specific individuals later on.

TAGGING SOMEONE IN A PHOTO

To mention someone in a photo, adhere to these steps:

1. Click on the image where you want to add a tag.
2. Press and hold the "Tag" button.
3. Enter the name of the person you want to tag.

4. Choose or press "Done."
5. The person will now be identified in the photo.
6. They will receive a notification informing them that they have been tagged.

SCAN DOCUMENTS WITH ONEDRIVE FOR BUSINESS

One advantageous capability provided by OneDrive for Business is the ability to utilize your smartphone's camera for scanning physical documents. This proves especially beneficial for scanning crucial papers like business cards or invoices.

Here's a step-by-step guide on how to scan a document:

1. Open the OneDrive for Business application on your smartphone.
2. Tap and hold the "+" symbol.
3. Select "Scan."
4. Place the paper you intend to scan on a flat surface.
5. Choose "Scan" to initiate the scanning process.

NB: Once the document is scanned, the application will convert it into a Portable Document Format (PDF).

6. Finally, you can either distribute or store the scanned file as needed.

Customize your scan

Tailoring your scan" refers to the process of adjusting a scan to meet your specific requirements or preferences. This involves modifying parameters such as pixel count, data format, speed, and the scanner's color mode, whether it's set to monochrome or grayscale. Additionally, customization may involve specifying which areas to scan or establishing automatic file naming conventions.

Including text in your scans is a useful practice for providing a document with a title or summary. Furthermore, the option to append text to each scan is crucial for providing documents with distinctive identities or overviews. Additionally, the option to enhance your scan by incorporating a watermark is available. This can be advantageous for including a recognition mark or your business logo within the document.

Documents can be organized and retrieved based on factors such as title, category, description, time period, or scope. Instead of downloading files to your device, the "Files on Demand" feature allows users to preview them directly.

When scanning documents, you have the option to customize various settings, including:

1. Scan speed: This setting determines the speed at which a document is digitally captured.
2. Resolution: This parameter defines the quality and sharpness of the scanned image.
3. File format: Specifies the type of file generated by the scanner, such as Portable Network Graphics (PNG), Joint Photographic Experts Group (JPEG), Tagged Image File Format (TIFF), or Portable Document Format (PDF).
4. Color mode: Indicates whether the scan should be performed in color or monochrome.
5. Dots per inch (DPI): This metric represents the image resolution, influencing the level of detail in the scan.
6. Auto optimization: This feature automatically adjusts the size of the image to fit predefined criteria.

SHARE LINK EXPIRATION

An expiration link is a shared link with a predetermined validity period, after which it becomes invalid. This feature serves various purposes. For instance, you may need to share a file temporarily for a specific task or meeting. In such cases, you can set the expiration date to coincide with the conclusion of the work or session. This ensures that once the specified period elapses, the file will no longer be accessible, providing security against perpetual access. Setting an expiration date is also a useful cybersecurity measure. You have several options for specifying the expiration date of your shared links, including one day, seven days, thirty days, or sixty days. Alternatively, you can choose to leave the expiration date blank to keep the share link active indefinitely.

To establish an expiration date for a share link, follow these instructions:

1. Choose the document you want to share by selecting the "Share" link.
2. Opt for "More options."
3. Navigate to "Link settings."
4. Click on "Settings for link expiration."
5. Specify the desired time frame for the link's validity.
6. Click the "OK" button.
7. Subsequently, you can provide the intended recipient with the share link.

SHARE LINK THAT REQUIRES A PASSWORD TO ACCESS

A "password-protected share link" is a URL initially shared with specific users, requiring a password to access the material or data linked at the URL. This feature is commonly used to limit access to specific individuals or organizations or to share confidential or sensitive data securely. This type of link adds an extra layer of security to users' files, as only those with the correct login credentials can access the content. It's crucial because the login information is the only means of gaining entry to the file. Moreover, it's a strategic choice for managing access to documents, allowing users to restrict file access to selected individuals using the password they set.

Follow these steps to create a share link with password protection:

1. Choose the document you want to share by clicking the "Share" icon.
2. Select "Advanced options."
3. Navigate to "Link settings."
4. Choose "Require a password."
5. Enter your preferred password.
6. Click "Confirm."
7. Once you input your login details, the sharing link will be generated.
8. The recipient can access the data by selecting "Join."

THE PERSONAL VAULT

Within OneDrive for Business, there exists a feature known as the "personal vault," providing users with a dedicated space to secure private documents. This area within your OneDrive for Business account demands additional authentication, such as a fingerprint or passcode, to gain access. It serves as a suitable option for storing sensitive documents like bank statements, tax records, and medical information.

Setting up the personal vault is a straightforward process:

- Click on the "Me" icon in the OneDrive for Business application.
- Select "Settings" and then choose "Personal vault."
- Click "Set up" and follow the provided instructions to configure your personal vault.
- Users will need to provide additional verification, such as a fingerprint or password.

Once configured, you can add documents to the personal vault using the same process as any other directory in OneDrive for Business.

Benefits of the personal vault:

1. It provides an additional layer of security as extra authentication, such as a password and a fingerprint, is required for access.
2. The contents of the personal vault are not easily discoverable, making it more challenging for unauthorized individuals to locate them.

VERSION HISTORY

The "version history" feature in OneDrive for Business allows users to track and review a file's entire history of modifications. If needed, users can also restore a previous version of their document. OneDrive for Business's version history function records every change made to a file, including the creation date, modification date, and author of each modification.

To access the version history, follow these steps:

- Click on the file for which you want to view the version history.
- Select the "File" icon located in the upper-right corner of the interface.
- Choose "Version history" from the "File" submenu.
- A list of the file's versions will be displayed.
- Users can examine or restore a version by clicking on its details.

HOW TO RESTORE A PREVIOUS VERSION?

Follow these steps to revert a file to an earlier state:

1. Navigate to the version you want to restore by selecting it from the version history panel.
2. Choose "Restore" from the menu.
3. A confirmation message will appear in a dialog box asking if you want to proceed with the restoration.
4. Click "Restore" to confirm.
6. The file will be reverted to the selected backup version.
   It's important to note that when you restore a document, the current version will be replaced by the selected backup version.

Additional details on version history:

When working on a document in OneDrive for Business's online version, the version history will only show changes made in the online version. Modifications made in the desktop version will not be visible. Additionally, only certain file types, such as Word, Excel, and

PowerPoint files, support version history. Not all file types can utilize this feature. Lastly, version history can be enabled or disabled for each individual file. Disabling it may be beneficial if you prefer not to track changes made to the file.

Save your document to your device or OneDrive

You have the option to save your document either to your OneDrive account or to your smartphone. Saving a file on your device means storing it temporarily on the device you're using. This is a practical choice if you want to edit the document offline or need offline access to its content. On the other hand, saving a file on OneDrive keeps it securely stored in a centralized location. This is a wise decision if you plan to share the content with others or require access to the file across multiple platforms. Additionally, you can choose to store a file on both OneDrive and your smartphone or tablet for added flexibility.

Advantages of Saving Documents on Your Device

1. Your documents remain accessible even without an internet connection.
2. You have more control over where your data is stored.
3. Stored documents remain available even if OneDrive encounters technical issues.
4. Users can free up space in their OneDrive account by saving specific documents on their device.
5. It's easy to transfer documents across different devices.
6. Users can conveniently save files to a removable disk.

Advantages of Saving Documents in OneDrive

1. Continued accessibility of your files during internet outages.
2. More control over determining where your files are stored.
3. Files remain accessible even if OneDrive experiences disruptions in service.
4. You can select specific documents to save on your device, freeing up space in your OneDrive account.
5. Effortless relocation of documents across various devices.
6. Easy storage of documents on a separate hard drive for security purposes.

EMBED FILES ON YOUR WEBSITE

What does embedding files on your website entail?

Embedding involves placing a file on your website to enable user access. This method is advantageous if you aim to provide users with access to files, presentations, or other documents directly on your website. By integrating files within the webpage, users can import or view them within their web interface. Incorporating files into your website is a straightforward way to share content with your audience and works seamlessly. It's also possible to embed documents from cloud storage services like OneDrive.

Embedding a file from OneDrive is relatively simple. Begin by locating the specific folder, then copy its sharing link. Create a new page on your website and insert the sharing link into the webpage markup. Once done, saving the template will effectively embed your file. It's that straightforward! However, ensure that your webpage visitors have the necessary application to open the attachment and that you have obtained the appropriate permissions to include it.

Embedding files on your website has both advantages and disadvantages. One advantage is that it provides easy access for visitors without requiring them to download the files. Another benefit is the convenience of updating the file without the need to update the website. However, a notable disadvantage is that if the file is removed from OneDrive, it becomes inaccessible on your website. Furthermore, if a visitor has a slow internet connection, it may result in a longer loading time for the file.

When embedding a file from OneDrive, it's crucial to consider that the file becomes accessible to anyone with the sharing link. This implies that you should only embed files that you are comfortable sharing with the public. Additionally, be mindful that others could copy or download the file. If security is a concern, you might want to explore alternative methods for sharing your files.

RESTORE YOUR ONEDRIVE

To put it simply, restoring your OneDrive involves reverting your account to a previous state. This option is particularly useful if you accidentally deleted a document or need to undo any changes made to your account. You have the flexibility to restore individual documents or your entire data from OneDrive, with the ability to specify the date and time for restoration.

However, it's important to note that OneDrive restoration is only possible up to a point prior to your last data backup. Let's start with the basics:

Microsoft OneDrive is a cloud storage solution that allows users to store documents online and access them from any device. OneDrive offers a range of features, including document sharing, collaboration tools, and scheduled backups, all available for free with a Microsoft account. Users can also opt to upgrade to a paid plan for additional services and extra storage space.

To begin the restoration process, log into your OneDrive account and navigate to the "Settings" page. From there, select the "Restore your OneDrive" link, which will take you to a screen where you can schedule the start date and time for the OneDrive restoration. You also have the option to choose whether to restore specific documents or your entire OneDrive data. Once you've made your selection, click "Restore."

Please note that the duration of this process may vary depending on the amount of data you're attempting to recover.

INDEX

restricted, 11

www.ingramcontent.com/pod-product-compliance
Lightning Source LLC
LaVergne TN
LVHW081532050326
832903LV00025B/1751